THE

Sex

APPEAL

⟨≈⟩

CELEBRATING SEXUAL PURITY IN A GODLY WAY

⟨≈⟩

Foreword By Praise Fowowe

THE
Sex
APPEAL

Celebrating Sexual Purity
In a Godly Way

Anthony Cute Amalokwu

Foreword by Praise Fowowe

Cute Edge™ Publishers, Lagos-Nigeria

iii

The Sex Appeal
Copyright © 2010 by Anthony Cute Amalokwu
Foreword Copyright © 2010 by Praise Fowowe

Published by:
Cute Edge™ Publishers
1, Balogun Street, Kuje-Amuwo,
Amuwo-Odofin, Lagos, Nigeria.
Tel: 07092293865, 08023220158

National Library of Nigeria Cataloguing in Publication Data
A CIP record for this book is available from the
National Library of Nigeria

ISBN 978-978-902-881-8

Design by: Oluwatosin Adeniyi, Eureka Productions
Illustrated by: Olawale Oyeola

Unless otherwise indicated, all scripture quotations are taken
from the authorized King James Version (KJV)

First Edition

DEDICATION

To my wonderful wife, Vicky

To my soldiers, Daniela, Emmanuel and Ozioma

To all involved in the campaign against
HIV/AIDS

ACKNOWLEDGEMENT

I give all the glory to God for giving me the inspiration to write this book. I am indeed grateful, Lord.

For being a source of motivation and also for encouraging me to start putting my thoughts into writing, I appreciate you - Pastor Mark Osereme.

To my wife – Imaobong and my very active soldiers – Daniela, Emmanuel and Ozioma Amalokwu, thank you for providing an enabling environment to write this book. You are really my love, a gift and bundle of joy from God.

To Pastor Remi Morgan for his fatherly and professional counsel and to my wonderful and cheerful sister - Lillian Nnanna, Ms. Iddy Oga-Palmer and Pastor Praise Fowowe, thank you for sharing with me the burden of editing and reviewing of this book. You made the needed finishing touches to this book possible.

To the entire church office team at R.C.C.G – Glorious Liberty Assembly – especially Sister Joy Nwaoha and Brother Chukwuemeka Echewa who did most of the typing of my manuscript, thank you for facilitating my vision of becoming an author.

TABLE OF CONTENTS

FOREWORD

When the truth about sex is not discovered lies will be taught from one generation to the other. We live in a world that some people have described as a sexualized world where the ages of sexual initiation among our young people have dropped to an all time low of 8years yet most of us saddled with the responsibility of teaching the right values about sex shy away from it.

The parents hardly discuss it, the churches wouldn't talk about it and the government doesn't even have what to say to our young minds yet a statistical projection says if nothing is done 75million Nigerians would be living with HIV by 2020. The question is what have we done?

Sex is everywhere at the moment but the truth about sex has become very scarce. That is why this book is a timely wake-up call and an indispensible resource material for every home in a world whose continued existence is threatened by the HIV/AIDS scourge.

Pastor Anthony Amalokwu has done a great job in this easy to read masterpiece on the subject of sexuality. His definitions of biblical truths on sexuality got me glued to the book and his mastery of the subject of HIV/AIDS is highly commendable.

I have read this book over and over again and I want you to know that if you love and value your family and the future of the family system then you can't afford not to read this book with your family. If 75million Nigerians would not live with HIV by 2020 then this book is a must read for all.

Get blessed and may your eyes of understanding be opened as the truth about sex and sexuality is laid bare once again by Pastor Tony.

Praise O. Fowowe
Author, Undressing Sex

INTRODUCTION

Ignorance is costly...

I was deeply touched by the ordeal of an innocent woman, faithful though she was who died of HIV/AIDS which she contracted from her husband. Sadly, he confessed to have acquired the said disease from a one-night stand. Beatrice's story (not her real name) is the inspiration for this book.

The scourge of Human Immunodeficiency Virus (HIV) in our world today, especially in third world countries, thrives on ignorance, high level of immorality and sexual perversion. Ignorance about HIV/AIDS has increased the level of prejudice and discrimination against its victims.

Stories abound of infected persons becoming homeless, finding their belongings on the street and their homes locked against them; of children barred from school; workers fired; and many other forms of indignities. I have also heard of some organizations that subtly make their infected staff redundant as an excuse to fire them. These companies apart from not employing persons that tested positive during their initial employment medical tests carry out periodic medical tests on employees.

It is easy to point accusing fingers at such organizations but the question is, "would you act differently?" While they may have a reason for their actions, there is also a need to strike a balance and give a human face to how we treat victims of HIV/AIDS who are seeking employment or are already employed.

The story of an infected pastor who lost his wife to AIDS and is still saving souls through his ministry to both the uninfected and those living with HIV/AIDS, will help us change our attitude towards those victims of the deadly disease. Whether it was by accident or their fault that they got infected is not a good enough ground to condemn them. Our Lord Jesus said "let him that hath no sin cast the first stone". Jesus has given us a ministry of reconciliation and not that of condemnation.

This book is not intended to condemn those who got infected through any of the above condemned behaviours and are now living with HIV or those currently involved in these sexual perversions. The purpose of this book is to inform them that God still loves them. He loves us even while we are in sin or down with sickness.

Satan is the killer but God through His son Jesus with outstretched arm is waiting for us to come back to Him for every help and comfort that we need. There is hope for us all when we forsake darkness and embrace God's light. God has kept you alive to turn over a new leaf and be reconciled to His eternal purpose for you.

If you are wondering why God has not destroyed today's world as He did to Sodom and Gomorrah, it is because He cannot play into the hands of Satan who desires more human beings to die in their sins and join him with his fallen angels in the lake of fire.

Turn these pages, and let's discover together how Satan is employing sexual perversions as strategic warfare weapons against the purpose of God for our lives. It will amaze you to learn of how much incursion Satan has made into humanity, corrupting the beautiful creations of God. When you are through, you will agree with me that without the help of God to uphold and guide us in our daily life, man is capable of being corrupted.

Part One

DEFINING THE TERMS

The Sex Appeal

CHAPTER ONE

─────∽─────

WHAT IS
LASCIVIOUSNESS?

*...who being past feeling have giving themselves
over unto lasciviousness, to work all uncleanness
with greediness" Eph. 4:17-19.*

POP-UPS...

Sometimes back, I bought a CDMA telephone because of its lower tariffs and it was very useful to my family at home. With the introduction of dial-up internet services, the phone became even more valuable as I could go online in the comfort of my home.

Late one night, while I was using the internet service on the computer system in our bedroom, the unthinkable happened! Right there before my eyes were high definition photographs of nude women and other clips of men and very physically endowed women having sex.

I immediately looked back to my wife on the bed wondering what she will say if she caught me

watching those videos. Thank God, she was fast asleep. She would have been much confused if she saw her dear husband, a man of God, looking at those photographs. Personally, I felt much defiled, though a married man.

I spoke to an IT fellow who said I needed to block those pop-ups but I was so harassed by those images and felt the only reasonable step was to suspend my subscription to the internet service. It helped my peace of mind and got me thinking of what could possibly be happening at our public cyber cafes especially when our teenagers go for night browsing or alone with their internet ready laptop computers. It must be reiterated that parents must pay more attention to the type of materials their children have access to in order to guide them appropriately. This is necessary due to the rate of sexual perversion in the society.

Sexual perversion

Sexual sin encompasses several forms of perversions like:

* Incest (Lev.20:12, 1Cor.5:1),

- Bestialism (Lev.18:23),
- Lesbianism (Rom.1:24-26),
- Homosexualism or sodomy (Rom.1:27-29),
- Harlotry (1Cor.6:13-18),
- Adultery (Matt.5:32),
- Fornication (1Cor. 7:2) and
- Idolatry (2Chr.21:11, Isa.41:29).

———❧———

...the sin which attempts to corrupt or truncate His divine purpose and order incurs stiffer penalty.

———❧———

Satanic wisdom births confusion and every evil work. The god of this age has manipulated and blinded the eyes of men, such that, man's understanding is so darkened that Sodom and Gomorrah sounds like a child's play compared to the level of sexual perversions practiced today, even among Christians.

Divine order...

"The world that was" became chaotic (confused) because of Lucifer's rebellion. That pre-Adamite world was empty and confused until God by His Spirit moved upon the face of the chaotic earth. He established order as "the heavens and earth which now is" was re-created. God demands order and through His word (Isa. 28:13) establishes order in Heaven and on earth. Inhabitants of heaven and earth are all subject to God's order and any attempt to introduce confusion by any of His creation incur His wrath and judgment.

God does not leave unpunished any sin and the sin which attempts to corrupt or truncate His divine purpose and order incurs stiffer penalty.

> *"And the angels which kept not their first estate, but left their own habitation, He hath reserved in everlasting chains under darkness unto the judgment of the great day. Even as Sodom and Gomorrah, and the cities about them in like*

24

manner, giving themselves over to fornication, and going after strange flesh, are set   forth for an example, suffering the vengeance of eternal fire" Jude 6-7.

God reserved Satan and all his fallen angels unto the judgment of the great day but He made a special case of the set of fallen angels who committed fornication with human beings. While Satan and some other fallen angels are still roaming free as principalities, powers, dominions, princes of darkness and demons, the ones who lived contrary to nature (God's order) by breaking through the sex bounds that God has set for them are bound in chains until the great white throne judgment (2Pet. 2:4. Rev.20:11-15).

These angels in chains did not remain in their own realm but entered the human realm and married the daughters of men in an attempt to do away with pure Adamite stock and thus prevent the seed of the woman from coming into the world to defeat them (Gen. 6:1-4). The angels like Sodom and Gomorrah lived contrary to nature and committed fornication.

The sexual perversion of Sodom and Gomorrah was contrary to nature, as it is contrary to God's order for men to become homosexuals. All forms of sexual perversions including incest, bestialism, lesbianism, homosexualism, fornication, adultery and sex between angels and women is total

CONFUSION as they are all contrary to nature or God's order.

Lasciviousness...

Lasciviousness is a word used to describe a group of words. It is translated from the Greek word 'Aselgeia' which means 'Licentiousness, lustfulness, unchastity and lewdness' It can be described as, "Promoting or Partaking of that which tends to produce lewd emotions, anything tending to foster sex and lust." It is the absence of restraint, indecency, wantonness and shameless conduct.

> *"This I say therefore, and testify in the Lord, that ye henceforth work not as other Gentiles walk, in the vanity of their mind, having the understanding darkened, being alienated from the life of God through the ignorance that is in them, because of the blindness of their heart: who being past feeling have giving themselves over unto lasciviousness, to work all uncleanness with greediness" Eph. 4:17-19.*

The above scripture captures the cause of all the sexual sins called lasciviousness. The natural man without Jesus does not have the life of God. He therefore walks in vanity, darkened understanding, ignorance and greediness all due to the blindness of the heart.

> *"In whom the god of this world hath blinded the minds of them which believe not, lest the light of the glorious gospel of Christ, who is the image of God, should shine unto them." 2Cor. 4:4.*

Dr. ED Murphy in his book 'The Hand Book for Spiritual Warfare' said, "Maintaining a truly moral life in today's sexually saturated culture is really spiritual warfare." Sex in all forms is the fastest selling product in the world today such that sexually suggestive advert campaigns are now used even in the marketing of consumer products that has nothing to do with sex.

Shameless conduct...

Lasciviousness is also shameless conduct. It is the promoting or partaking of that which tends to produce lewd emotions; anything tending to foster sex sin and lust. It is any shameful act perpetrated in darkness that is also disgusting to the offender when discussed or brought to the open. The boldness with which these acts are perpetrated disappears whenever the matter is brought to the light.

All men without the fear of God have the potential to act shamelessly; even the much respected and revered "Men of God." Therefore, it is crucial that members pray for their Pastors, otherwise, even a small girl empowered by Satan can totally destroy their lives and ministry.

I remember the story of a pastor who after 5 years of marriage without a child impregnated a worker in the same Church. Worse, he immediately resigned as a Pastor with a note to the Church saying, "I am resigning, take the Church and the wife you gave me." Undoubtedly, this Pastor must

have been unfaithful to his wife. He was an adulterer before he impregnated the member and remained an adulterer after leaving the Church and the wife of his youth to go away with the pregnant lady. He had a calling to Pastor and not to sleep with his Church members. It is only a shameless and wicked shepherd that butchers and eats the sheep he is meant to protect (Ez.34:1-10).

—❧—

All men without the fear of God have the potential to act shamelessly; even the much respected and revered "Men of God."

—❧—

Satan is waging war against the Church through members. Some say the men of God are to blame but I say both the church members and the Pastors involved are to blame for being unaware of the devices of Satan. I also remember the story of a supposed man of God who was sleeping with pre-teenagers, teenagers and almost all the female members of his choir.

One of his victims narrated her ordeal of how she became a sex toy of the false prophet.

—❧—

It is shameful for a child to see his father's nakedness. Do we not call our Pastors, 'father in the Lord'?

—❧—

She said she was invited to the prophet's room to be briefed on her new appointment in the 'Word and

31

Sound' department. On getting there, she met the prophet half naked but was told not to be afraid. However, in the course of discussion, he started to make unimaginable sexual demands. When I heard the story, I was struck by her naivety as any mature

woman would have taken to her heels on meeting the General Overseer half naked.

It is shameful for a child to see his father's nakedness. Do we not call our Pastors, 'father in the Lord'? To see our father's nakedness is a curse, even if he is drunk with lust. We must protect our Pastor from Satan's attack otherwise the flock will scatter. Let us strongly fight Satan who is winning the battle against families. After all, a girl with a good family upbringing will not see her Pastor's nakedness and remain there even when the Pastor tells her it is okay to do so.

> *"And Ham, the father of Canaan, saw the nakedness of his father, and told his two brethren. And shem and Japheth took a garment, and laid it upon both their shoulders, and went backward, and covered the nakedness of their father, and their faces were backward, and they saw not their fathers nakedness And Noah awoke from his wine, and knew what his younger son had done unto him. And he said, cursed be Canaan, a servant of servants shall he be unto his brethren". Gen 9: 22-25*

Likewise, I have heard of shameless conducts in homes. I remember the tale of Jane (not her real name) who came for counseling concerning the harassment she was facing at home from her elder

33

sister's husband. She said her brother-in-law was so shameless that he would make passes at her even in the presence of her sister. Eventually, her sister did noticed and confronted Jane.

Shortly, the harassment intensified as the brother-in-law would sneak into her room and try to fondle her. When she awakes, he would run as fast as he

could into the sitting room and sit quietly in the dark. She never told her sister for fear that the shameless conduct of her husband could break their marriage. She desires to pack out of her sister's house but is scared of what her sister will make of her decision.

I counseled that Jane should tell her sister her story and seek her opinion on both sisters. Wisdom, I

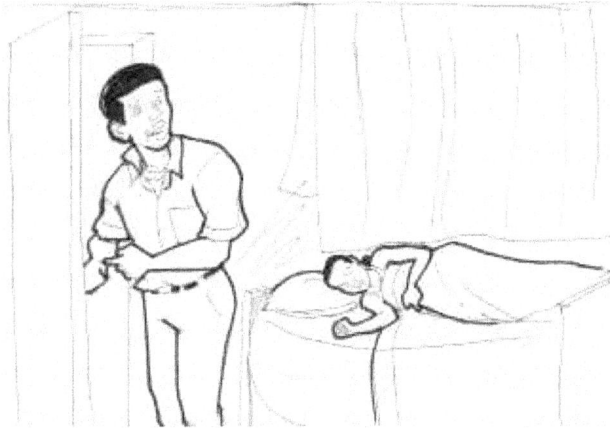

trust, will guide her to know how to present her ordeal to the elder sister. It is paramount she does tell her sister first before she is framed by her brother-in-law. Who do you think the wife will believe? Your guess is as good as mine.

Without Christ and His grace, we are all vulnerable

to evil devices. Hence, Jesus Christ is the only way out for the brother-in-law. It is only Christ who can save the brother-in-law and deliver him from temptations. With God's grace, in addition to being born again, he can even become a pastor who could use his past experiences to preach to others.

Wantonness

In addition, Lasciviousness is also described as wantonness. A wanton person is sexually unbridled, promiscuous and uncontrolled; he is indifferent to the needs of others. A particular fellow comes to mind, Kelvin (not real name). He is definitely the most wanton fellow I know. Even though he is rich and young, no family in his village would give their daughter to him in marriage because of his notoriety.

It was recounted that while Kelvin was on his way to a night party in his village, he was beaten by rain. Luckily, the younger sister of his bosom friend agreed to escort him back home with an umbrella so he could change his clothes.

Somehow, he managed to get the girl into his room to wait for him while he changed into a new set of clothes. Alas, he tried to sleep with the girl. When she refused and reminded him that she was his friend's sister, he replied "it is even better to keep it in the family." Kelvin would have raped that girl but for the timely intervention of his elder sister.

Back in the city where he eventually settled, he continued his philandering ways until one of his numerous girlfriends was able to tie him down in marriage. Perhaps, she ignorantly assumed that marriage was the much needed reformation that Kelvin needed.

———— ❧ ————

Wantonness is in the flesh and a carnal man cannot overcome it by his strength.

———— ❧ ————

After several years of childlessness, it was discovered that Kelvin had low sperm count. The wife spent her money to buy him several herbal

products like GLND or TIANSHI to boost his sperm count. Sadly, when she finally took in after 8 years of marriage, she lost the baby due to a veneral disease contracted from her husband. She is very miserable today and if she had known she would not have married a wanton man.

Wanton fellow, regardless of how much we want them to change, cannot change except they receive the life of God by surrendering to Jesus Christ. Wantonness is in the flesh and a carnal man cannot overcome it by his strength.

CHAPTER TWO

WHAT IS LEWDNESS?

"You have heard that it was said,
"You shall not commit adultery" but I say to you,
that everyone who looks on a woman to lust for her has
committed adultery with her already in his heart". Matt. 5:27-28.

Longman's family dictionary defines lewdness as obscene, salacious or sexually coarse or suggestive. We can classify male sexual dominance, video seduction through TV's and internet or print media pornography as lewdness.

Male Sexual Dominance

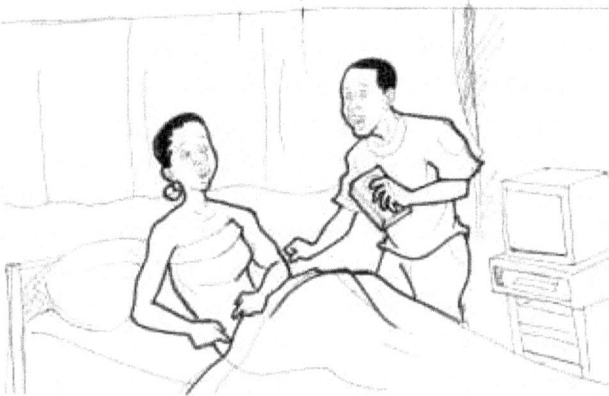

This describes the activity of men who coerce their wives to participate in sexual practices repulsive to the woman's usually more refined nature. It is a sin against God and against one's wife. It is an unrestrained illicit sexual behavior without concern for the feelings of others, in this case one's wife.

Some men including Christian leaders have done permanent damage to their wives by this male sexual dominance.

There was a case of Mr. Elvis (not real name), an elder in church from a dysfunctional family who was married to a beautiful, pure, gentle girl from a stable Christian family. Mr. Elvis' sexual appetite was voracious. He not only wanted sex continually but wanted his wife to be more passionate and do things that were repulsive to her. He began to rent x-rated videos and compelled her to look at them. When asked why she submitted to it? She said, "Because I love him and was afraid to lose him". This is the most common reason given by this type of sexually abused wife.

Some men including Christian leaders have done permanent damage to their wives by this male sexual dominance.

Soon the videos became less repulsive to her. Eventually she became dependent upon the explicit sexual acts of the videos to become aroused. In time, her self-esteem and her sense of female purity became so violated that she went into deep depression and almost committed suicide.

It took God's tender grace and transforming power to rescue both her and her husband from the pit into which they had pulled each other. Today they are in love anew and enjoy a tender love life free from the bondage to such sexual perversion.

VIDEO SEDUCTION (PORNOGRAPHY)

The scriptures are clear that immorality is committed in the eyes, mind and imagination before it is committed with the body. In the Sermon on the Mount, Jesus taught,

> *"You have heard that it was said, "You shall not commit adultery" but I say to you, that everyone who looks on a woman to lust for her has committed adultery with her already in his heart". Matt. 5:27-28.*

Jesus is saying that if one looks lustfully at a woman, he is guilty of adultery. This is immorality of the heart, of the mind, of the imagination. Living as we are in a world in which nudity, partial nudity and sexual stimulating dress style is rampant; the battle for mental purity for the child of God is more intense than ever.

One of Satan's primary instruments for sexual attack against the mind of humanity, usually men in general and believers in particular, is pornography.

It covers all forms of external physical tools which produce sexual arousal in those who use them.

———∽———

Living as we are in a world in which nudity, partial nudity and sexual stimulating dress style is rampant; the battle for mental purity for the child of God is more intense than ever.

———∽———

In Nigeria, pornography is gaining grounds into our culture and homes, especially with the availability of laptop computers with internet access and proliferation of cyber cafes; where our children have limitless access to x-rated sites and materials. Almost every street has a video shop where countless titles of pirated and cheap pornographic (x-rated) CDs and DVDs are sold.

I once queried my barber who owns one of these outlets on why he had to sell/lend these films to children and he replied, "Pastor, who told you they are children, there are no more children in this our neighborhood, before they start growing breast, they are already spoilt"

He said, "they start by buying for their parents, now they buy for themselves and I am in business to make money".

Sexually explicit books, many with pictures of nude male and female are available for children and adults in most book stands. The media, especially magazines, movies, videos and T.V. promote nudity and illicit sexual activities at an alarming rate.

Pornography, like prostitution has its own victims. They are everywhere. Pornography stimulates the imagination to commit mental adultery including masturbation. It stirs the passion and sexual arousal, especially of men, which makes them potentially dangerous to women and children.

———— ∽ ————

"Pastor, who told you they are children, there are no more
children in this our neighborhood, before they start growing
breast, they are already spoilt"
———— ∽ ————

Several cases abound of many men, including
Christians, who having been sexually stimulated by
pornography have sought sex anywhere even with
unwilling women or children. How much incest and
rape is due to sexual arousal stimulated by
pornography! Also, pornography is an aid to
masturbation whether it is mental or actual.

God designed marital sex to flow out of the context of a loving and intimate relationship where nurturing, communication, serving and tenderness exist. Sexual intercourse then becomes an expression of care, of love and a way of saying, "You matter to me, I love you and I want to communicate that to you tenderly."

I remember vividly the case of a young man who came to his pastor for deliverance prayers. He was tormented every night by beautiful women who came to have sex with him in his dreams; he wakes up with his clothes soiled. After the first deliverance session, there was no improvement.

During the second deliverance session, God instructed the pastor to enquire from the young man if he read magazines with pictures of nude women and he said "yes".

"How can you continue to read those kinds of

magazines and expect a miracle in this sessions?" the pastor replied. The young man created the dreams he was having through his exposures to pornographic materials.

Before we close this session, I want to recount the story of a Christian leader in America who fell into the trap of video pornography. It began innocently enough, with the gift of a video cassette recorder meant to be used to enhance his ministry.

At first, he and his family viewed only Disney classics. However, as he browsed for more family movies at the video shop, an exciting selection of fast action adventure movies caught his eyes. So in

50

addition to the family-type of movie, he would choose one of a more mature theme for him and his wife to enjoy after the children went to bed.

He enjoyed the action in these films, but doubts nibbled at him when actors swore, or the scantily clad actresses and actors engaged in scenes portraying sexual immorality. One day the suggestive picture and title on the CD case lured him to rent an R-rated picture. Soon he was watching two of these movies every weekend, then mid-week too.

He observed that, "although I continued my personal devotions out of habit, I knew that my reading of scripture and prayer were a sham. My enthusiasm for teaching and preaching the bible waned. I lost boldness in speaking on the bible commands against sexual immorality."

In spite of the determination not to view R-rated movie, the sensuous titles and alluring pictures drew him to view these movies week after week. Only his wife's moral sensitivity and presence in the home kept him from renting the X-rated movies he yearned to see.

Eventually, his wife went away for a weekend and at the video shop he justified his rental of X-rated movie by rationalizing, "perhaps as a Christian leader I should be aware of what the world is consuming".

Thankfully, what he saw in the movie disgusted him. 'What I saw was ugly," he said "the film degraded men and women. The beauty of sex as designed by God and experienced in my marriage was absent. I felt empty, cheated and defeated".

———&———

How much incest and rape is due to sexual arousal stimulated by pornography!

———&———

Shocked into realizing he was in danger of destroying his life and his ministry, that night he destroyed his video rental card, wrote a note of confession to his wife, repented before the Lord, and decided before God to stay out of video shops. Later he made himself accountable to a respected pastor friend to monitor his spiritual life.

My Appeal...

I close this session of lasciviousness with a passionate appeal. If the reader has any involvement with pornography or auto sexuality (masturbation), please break the habit now.

• Find a prayer partner who will pray with you and encourage you.

> *"Confess your faults one to another, and pray one for another, that ye may be healed. The effectual fervent prayer of a righteous man availeth much". Jam. 5:16.*

• Find someone to whom you can become accountable, who will check up on you, to whom you can go when temptations attempt to take control.

If you are a casual user, cut off the practice now, completely. Guard what you see in movies and on TV and videos. Refuse to buy, look at or read any sexually stimulating literature.

If you are a casual user, cut off the practice now, completely. Guard what you see in movies and on TV and videos. Refuse to buy, look at or read any sexually stimulating literature.

Your bondage will only increase if you do not stop now, give your life or rededicate your life to our Lord and Saviour, Jesus Christ and get help now.

The freedom you will experience is worth the initial struggle. *"The son of man will set you free and you will be free indeed".*

I personally enjoy that freedom. It is worth more than all material good of this life.

The Sex Appeal

Part Two

DEFINING
THE ACT

The Sex Appeal

CHAPTER THREE

I WANT TO
MARRY A PASTOR

Marriage is honorable in all, and the bed undefiled,
but fornicators and adulterers God will judge. (Heb 13:4)

Have you ever tried asking a single sister what kind of man she wants for a husband? A very common answer you get is, "A God fearing man." By extension, but for fear of the responsibilities of the wife of a man of God, almost all ladies would love to marry a pastor. In some churches, it is even a major prerequisite that a believer be married before he is promoted to the office of a pastor.

Due to preference of pastors as husband materials by majority of sisters, some churches went further to forbid a pastor from marrying from his parish. Did they foresee the life drama that took place in one popular church in Nigeria when the pastor lost his wife? Pastor James (not real name) was a very successful pastor living with HIV.

Christians are fond of confirming God's approval of their marriage partners through dreams.

While still in his late thirties, he lost his wife to the disease unknown to the church members and most eligible single sisters scheming to become his next wife.

He was very committed to a fellowship of people living with HIV/AIDS he help to set up when they first discovered that his wife was HIV positive and he by extension was also infected. How the wife contracted HIV was unknown but she contracted it whilst they were still in the world as they got married as unbelievers.

Pastor James was doing a very great work in loving, comforting and restoring hope to those living with HIV/AIDS, especially in his church. Church members who came to him for counseling after contracting the disease were integrated into the fellowship of people living with HIV/AIDS (PLWHA) where they can get the love, understanding and care the society today is denying

them.

Christians are fond of confirming God's approval of their marriage partners through dreams. Although, God speaks through dreams, firstly, we need to be mature in the things of the Lord as some dreams could arise from the activities of the mind during the day. If a sister preoccupies her mind fantasizing about marrying her pastor for instance, she will definitely see herself getting married to the pastor in the dream. This was the dilemma of

Pastor James, as countless sisters who approached him for counseling ended up sharing with him how they saw themselves getting married to him in one dream or revelation. The man of God knew he had to do something very fast before the entire work of God in his hands goes up in flames.

He was already in a relationship with one of the sisters at the PLWHA fellowship and realized that the only way to put an end to the chaotic situation with dreaming sisters in his church was to declare

his status publicly.

It was a difficult decision but he would not allow Satan destroy the work of God in his church by keeping quiet. On a day dedicated to talk about HIV/AIDS, the pastor stood before the church and recounted the event that led to the wife's death. He told them of how they did not know of the wife's sickness on time; else, they would have managed it. He told them that he believed the death of the wife was for a purpose and encouraged members to go for voluntary HIV screening as prevention is less costly than cure. He informed the church that those infected could still live a normal life with adequate management, care and support from loved ones.

Finally, he announced his marriage engagement to a sister everybody knew in church, and members could swear that the sister lied about her contracting HIV just to marry the pastor. Unfortunately, HIV/AIDS does not show on the face! *A popular HIV campaign slogan in Pidgin English is: "AIDS no dey show for face-o!!!"*

CHAPTER FOUR

YOUNG AND FREELY WILLING

"Lest there be any fornicator, or profane person, as Esau, who for one morsel of meat sold his birth right" Heb 12:16

A story was told of a maid who was sleeping around. She would go after security men also called 'Mallams' within the area where she lived. Between her routine of taking the children to school and bringing them back and other house chores, she would make out time to familiarize herself with security men in their neighbourhood.

Since most of these Mallams had little in-built kiosks in the houses they guarded where they sell petty things; the maid, in a bid to partake freely of some of these petty items got trapped into illicit sexual rendezvous with one Mallam after the other. It was during this period that she contracted HIV unknown to her.

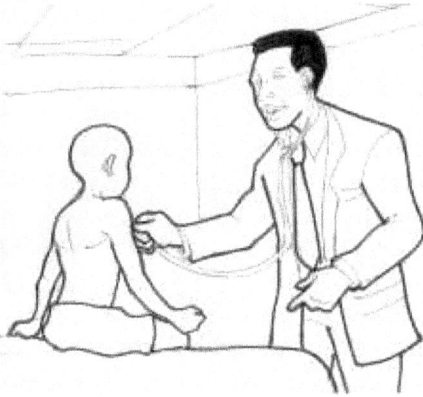

Not long after, one of her ward fell ill. He was treated for malaria parasite and there was no improvement. His blood sample was later collected to run a test. He tested positive to HIV virus and typhoid parasite. The parents became confused about his HIV status and the search for a possible explanation led to HIV screening of the entire household including the maid. The maid tested positive and so was their second child.

A deeper investigation into the source of the infection began and it was discovered that the maid was responsible. How? After series of interrogation and investigation into the lifestyle of the maid the truth emerged. She confessed to sleeping around. The confusion was not yet over. "Could she have slept with our son," they thought? But he is too small, they rationalized. What about our daughter? How did all these happen? These were the questions that went through their minds.

The doctor suggested that a possible way is through the sharing of blood piercing instruments like needles, razor blades or even tooth brush. The maid

later confessed to have been using the children's tooth brush to wash her teeth. "Oh! That is it" exclaimed the doctor, "bleeding gum and blood of the maid on the children's brush."

———◈———

We live in an era of wickedness perpetuated through a life of sexual perversion.

———◈———

You may say that was sheer carelessness but I will say, what wickedness! Were these parents careless? Well, even though there could have been an element of carelessness on the part of the parents, however, the cause of the tragedy is the wickedness and profanity of fornication.

Please note that although it is thought that HIV can be transmitted through sharing toothbrushes, no case of it has been documented medically except in this true life story. I have not come in contact with anyone who was infected via toothbrush. If we take a look at the virus perhaps you may understand.

The HIV virus has a short life outside of the body. A tooth brush is usually made of non-porous bristles making it hard for anything to stick. HIV needs body fluid for transmission. In this case blood and I think you would be able to spot a bloody toothbrush except out of share carelessness which may be possible in the above story.

Freebies

We live in an era of wickedness perpetuated through a life of sexual perversion. We must all repent. Repentance is a great gain to us and people around us. Longman family dictionary defines a "Prostitute as a person who engages in sexual practice for money." It went further to define Prostitution as the devotion of anything to corrupt or unworthy purposes.

---❦---

How easy it is to get people to believe you love them and to sell you their souls by giving them free things.

---❦---

Going by the first definition above, one is confused as to what to call a person who engages in sexual practices or offers his/her body for the use of another ex-gratia. This brings to mind another story of a young girl who thought it was fun to offer her body to willing men freely. She freely contracted HIV from one of her benefactors.

---❦---

She sold her birth right on a platter of sexual fantasy and wantonness.

---❦---

Her ordeal started as a teenager, out of secondary school and writing her JAMB (a pre-university qualification exam). She was at home most of the times alone; her parents would go to work and siblings to school. In the same compound of Room & Palour apartments (Face me, I face you), was a

71

young man who was into spare parts business.

The young business man saw a golden opportunity to sleep with this young girl while at home one day because he was down with Malaria fever. When he got better, he planned his battle strategy to seduce the innocent girl. He continually bought her gifts after their first meeting. These gifts were intended to seduce and hence could be called bribes.

"And thou shalt take no gifts: for gifts blindeth the wise, and perverteth the words of the righteous" Ex 23:8

How easy it is to get people to believe you love them and to sell you their souls by giving them free things. How we idolize the people who give us free things. It does not matter to us if the enjoyments of these free things are for a while (temporary) as long as it satisfies our immediate needs.

> *"Lest there be any fornicator, or profane person, as Esau, who for one morsel of meat sold his birth right" Heb 12:16*

A fornicator or adulterer is a profane person. Profanity is the treatment or abuse of something sacred, to desecrate or debase by an unworthy or improper use.

> *"…Now the body is not for fornication, but for the Lord; and the Lord for the body" ICor.6:13b.*

It was not long before the young businessman in our story trapped the girl and she lost her virginity! For the girl, the first experience was both painful

73

and sweet. It was easy for her to overcome the painful aspect and cling to the sweet aspect. Later, a married man in the same compound soon noticed her. She started sleeping with the married man. When she became the source of quarrel between the young businessman and the married man, she moved her search for fun (sexual pleasure) outside the compound. She failed her JAMB exams and was not bothered. She sold her birth right on a platter of sexual fantasy and wantonness. She could not stay a day without a man.

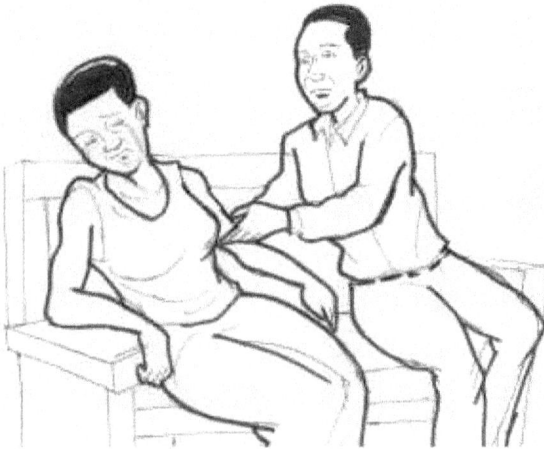

She continued in this madness until she fell sick with Malaria symptoms. She visited a government clinic where they took her blood samples to run a test. She was not just sick of Malaria Parasite but tested positive to HIV 1 and HIV 2 viruses. She was jolted to reality by the result of her HIV test. She was in counseling for over 2 hours and the doctor was trying to convince her that she could still live a normal life with the drugs available now. She could not stop crying over what she called a wasted life. She mortgaged her destiny.

> *"For you know how that afterwards, when he would have inherited the blessing, he was rejected: for he found no place of repentance, though he sought it carefully with tears"*
> *Heb 12:17.*

In a vengeful anger, the young girl told the doctor she has made up her mind to repay the men folk with their own coin. She vowed to no longer wait for men to approach her for sex but would embark

75

on a seduction mission first on all the men in her compound and then in her entire neighbourhood. It is free sex for all available men.

> *"Now is she without, now in the streets, and lieth in wait at every corner......with her much fair speech she caused him to yield, with the flattering of her lips she forced him"* Prov.7:12-21.

If this is exactly your story, the doctor is right and you could still live a normal life with immunosuppressant (antiretroviral) drugs. But if you found it difficult to believe the doctor and that is why you have embarked on that vengeance mission, I beg you to give the Doctor of all doctors, Jesus Christ, a chance to restore your life and destiny. Hear what He told Cain before he embarked on his vengeful mission:

> *"And the Lord said unto Cain, why art thou wroth? And why is thy countenance fallen? If thou doest well, shalt thou not be accepted? And if thou doest not well, sin lieth at the door. And unto thee shall be*

his desire, and thou shall rule over him" Gen 4:6-7.
Jesus came to this world and died for you. He came for the sinner and not the righteous. Sickness; HIV has its root in sin and your true repentance and confession of our Lord Jesus Christ as your saviour will orchestrate the free flow of His blood to wash and cleanse you, forgive and restore all that you may have lost.

> *"The thief cometh not, but for to steal, and to kill, and to destroy: I am come that they might have life, and that they might have it more abundantly" Jn. 10:10.*

Dearly beloved, if you have gone on this revenge mission for months or years, I challenge you to commit the same number of months or years in seeking Jesus. I did not say seeking a man of God but the greatest physician of all - Jesus. It is necessary that you find a complete Bible believing church in your area, but you must first surrender your life to Jesus, where ever you are right now and pray this prayer:

God Almighty Father, I accept that I am a sinner and Jesus came and died for me. I accept Jesus into my life today. Cleanse me with the blood of Christ and write my name in your book of life. I refuse every covenant I have with the devil, directly or indirectly, in Jesus' name.

You are now a born again Christian. What you need now is a Bible, the great book that God will use to lead you on. If you are a young girl and the above stories practically describes your situation only that you have not gone for HIV test, please proceed immediately for a free HIV test in any government health centre near you.

———

I beg you to give the Doctor of all doctors, Jesus Christ, a chance to restore your life and destiny.

———

Thereafter, you are also encouraged to follow the counsel given above, whether the result is negative or positive. That it is negative should make you forsake your old ways and run to Jesus to show gratitude for His love & protection.

The Sex Appeal

CHAPTER FIVE

———— ∽ ————

THE IDOLATER
(A LIFE WITHOUT GOD)

*"For thy maker is thine husband;
the LORD of hosts is His name; and thy redeemer
the Holy one of Israel; The God of the whole earth
shall He be called". Isa 54:5*

The root of prostitution and all forms of sexual perversion and wickedness is IDOLATRY.

We are by creation owned by God and by covenant married to Him. We are created to serve God and Him only. We are to put God first in all that we do, as putting Him second amounts to idolatry. Serving God in addition to other gods is also equivalent to idolatry.

> *"And they committed whoredoms in Egypt; they committed whoredoms in their youth... And*

82

Aholah played the harlot when she was mine;...Thus she committed her whoredoms with them, with all them that were the chosen men of Assyria, and with all on whom she doted: with all their idols she defiled herself". Ez. 23:3-7.

From the above scriptures, two sisters Samaria (Aholah) and Jerusalem (Aholibah) were guilty of whoring with Egypt, indicating the idolatry of Israel while in that land. They also whored in their youth against God who made the mosaic covenant with them and caused them to become His wife by covenant relationship.

The root of prostitution and all forms of sexual perversion and wickedness is IDOLATRY. Trust in man, man-made items, divination and all other forms of apostasy can incur the anger of God. The anger of God is revealed against all ungodly; these are those who do not live to reverence God.

83

> *Teaching us that, denying ungodliness and worldly
> lusts, we should live soberly, righteously, and godly,
> in this present world; looking for that blessed hope,
> and the glorious appearing of the great God and
> our Saviour Jesus Christ;..." Titus 2:12-14.*

Unrighteousness...

This includes having pleasure in wrong doers and
all acts of wrong doing; immorality, wickedness of
heart and life.

> *"Being filled with all unrighteousness, fornication,
> wickedness, covetousness, maliciousness, full of
> envy..." Rom.1:29-31.*

God's Anger

> *"For the invisible things of him from the creation of
> the world are clearly seen, being understood by the
> things that are made, even his eternal power and
> Godhead; so that they are without excuse:"
> Rom1:20*

There is now no need to entertain vain imaginations or be involved in unfruitful arguments to deny you of the grace of God. Some would argue that if Jesus Christ is the only way, then what will happen to our great forefathers who lived before the Law of Moses and the coming of our Lord Jesus Christ?

Are you that willing to continue in idolatry; a life of unthankfulness or ingratitude to your maker just because you would have preferred to live in the era of those who will be judged by conscience or law than this era of grace; the era of the gospel of Christ? Remember that just as your great forefathers are not excusable from God's anger (judgment) so also are you not if you chose to remain in idolatry.

> *"And if any man hear my words, and believe not, I judge him not... He that rejected me, and receiveth not my words, hath one that judgeth him: the word that I have spoken, the same shall judge him in the last day. Jn12:47-48*

85

Hallmarks of Idolaters...

> *"Because that, when they knew God, they glorified him not as God, neither were thankful; but became vain in their imaginations, and their foolish heart was darkened. Professing themselves to be wise, they became fools..."Rom1:21-23.*

You are idolatrous, ungodly and unrighteous when your daily actions do not glorify God. We must by our actions or way of life bestow honour, praise, and admiration unto God and cause men to do same. When you sleep and wake-up, go out and come in on a daily basis and you fail to find an avenue to express your gratitude to God, then you are an idolater. We must declare at least one day in a week to congregate with other children of God in fellowship to worship the Almighty God. We must serve God in the market place (business place, office, school, etc.) and must not forsake the fellowship of other believers (Heb.10:25).

—❧—

You are idolatrous, ungodly and unrighteous when your
daily actions do not glorify God.

—❧—

It is shocking to see human beings pursue money all
the days of a week even on the days they are

supposed to be in the presence of God. In addition
to time spent, we must spend physical cash, material
possessions, talents, gifts and ideas in showing
appreciation to our God.

> *"And God saw that the wickedness of man was great in the earth, and that every imagination of the thoughts of his heart was only evil c o n t i n u a l l y "*
> *Gen.6:5.*

Vain or evil imaginations are the lifestyle of an idolater. When you do any good thing for him, he interprets your actions to mean evil. If you give him a free drink for instance, he imagines you have poisoned it.

"To the defiled all things are defiled" Titus 1:15.

The heart of an idolater is dark. An evil heart is full of darkness just like a good heart is full of light (Matt.6:23). Thank God for His mercy, He does not derive pleasure in the death of a sinner. He gives idolaters extended time to come to repentance but they have capitalized on His longsuffering to continue in their evil ways.

"Because sentence against an evil work is not executed speedily, therefore the heart of the sons of men is fully set in them to do evil" Ecc.8:11

Imagine if in our world today, God is executing immediate judgment upon the wicked? The story would have been different. It would have been in Satan's favour. Why did I say to Satan's favour? It is Satan who wants people to die in their sins and wickedness so he can have more companions in the lake of fire. God did not create lake of fire for man but for Satan and his fallen angels.

An idolater is always wise in his own eyes. An idolater is therefore a fool. It is only a fool that says or acts as if there is no God. Demons know that there is God and they tremble before Him but idolaters who worship these demons are deceived to claim otherwise in their foolishness and ignorance.

An idolater substitutes the glory of our

incorruptible God in their mind with images of men, birds, dogs, frogs, snakes, etc. When they form their gods in human shape, they endow them with passions and present themselves as slaves to sex perversions and gratification.

CHAPTER SIX

HOMOSEXUALISM

For this cause, God gave them up to dishonorable affections.
For even their women changed the natural use into that
which is against nature. (Rom 1:26)

---◅◦▻---

Love, I counseled my friend, is the only weapon that can empower him to help the ladies.

---◅◦▻---

I never met a lesbian in my days as unbeliever. I am yet to meet a lesbian in counseling even now as a pastor. But do lesbians, the people God is describing in the above scripture, exist? Yes. Do they go to church? Yes. Are they born again Christians? Yes, some of them are "born again".

A friend once told me a story about some lesbians who live in the same compound with him and how he detest and put them at arm's length. I am sure a lot of Christians will react like my friend if they knew one too. The three lesbian ladies in my friend's compound each stay with their respective elder brothers. They attend one church or the other and participate regularly in devotion every morning with their relations. The activities of these girls came to the open one day, when a wife to one of the elder brother caught two of the ladies doing the abominable things.

My friend hoped that after the disgrace they would stop, but he was mistaken. God showed him how the activities of these women have brought a heavy aura of wickedness and evil in the entire compound. My friend continued to pray but to no avail. Love, I counseled my friend, is the only weapon that can empower him to help the ladies.

He was only transferring his hatred for the demon

93

of lesbianism to those ladies. This is what Satan wants to achieve so that deliverance and salvation could be hindered from flowing to them through him. I further counseled my friend to engage those demons of lesbianism in a power encounter by inviting the ladies one after the other for a friendly chat.

I gave him a step by step procedure, informed him of the existence of multiple personality in each of those ladies and how to handle the situation. I told him to take up the male of the three lesbian ladies as I felt the strongman controlling them must be resident in her.

As at the time of going to the press, the lady acting as the male is already born again to the glory of the Lord. My friend was so excited when he was sharing the testimony. However, the battle just began. My friend informed me that since the conversion of the male lesbian, the other two have been very unfriendly towards him for taking away their lover and introducing her to a better way of life.

I have also counseled him to isolate the female lesbian that looks stronger for the next encounter. This is necessary and urgent to avoid the transfer of the male lesbian demon personality to her. If that happens, they will become comfortable again and continue where they left off with our now born again sister.

Gay diagnosis...

"In June of 1981 we saw a young gay man with the most devastating immune deficiency we had never seen. We said, 'we don't know what this is, but we hope we don't ever see another case like it again'."

— Dr Samuel Broder, USA

In, 1979, two young men from New York City visited their doctors with symptoms of a rare tumour, Kaposi sarcoma which had been diagnosed in other young men in other cities in US. Also, there were cases of another rare disease - pneumocystis carinii pneumonia – which was also making appearance in various parts of the country. These cases took puzzled doctors a while to realize that these scattered mysteries were part of a trend.

What was causing these rare conditions in previously healthy young men? It fell on epidemiologists - or "medical detectives" - to piece together the picture. After much research, two facts linked the cases together: all the patients were homosexuals and their diseases indicated a drastically weakened immune system.

What mostly distinguished early AIDS patients (which for a short time in the USA was called gay-related immune deficiency- GRID) was their homosexuality, so scientists began looking for clues into their lifestyles.

The use of inhalant "poppers" - stimulant drugs based on amyl nitrite - was widespread in the sections of gay community in the United States of America at the time and scientists wondered whether these could have caused the men's immune system to collapse. The observation that AIDS was more common among men who had many sex partners, sexually transmitted diseases (STDs) and intestinal infections, led to a second theory that the men might be overburdening their immune systems to the point of collapse. Unexpected appearances of pneumocystis carinii pneumonia and Kaposi sarcoma among injecting drug users did nothing to undermine this hypothesis, as initially it was argued that hepatitis B and other infections caused by needle-sharing might similarly overload the immune system.

I once counseled a sister who left her husband (a pastor) after three years in marriage. Her story was that she had always believed God to marry a pastor. Therefore, when a young general overseer of a church approached her for her hand in marriage, she took it as prayer answered and got married to him.

She discovered after the wedding that the man of God was impotent and that he never told her during their courtship. To me, that was treacherous and should have rendered that marriage covenant null and void. However, the sister continued to endure and pray to God to heal the husband and make him whole again but to no avail.

> *And likewise also the men, leaving the natural use of the woman, burned in their lust toward one another; males with males working out shamefulness, and receiving in themselves the recompense which was fitting for their error. (Rom 1:27)*

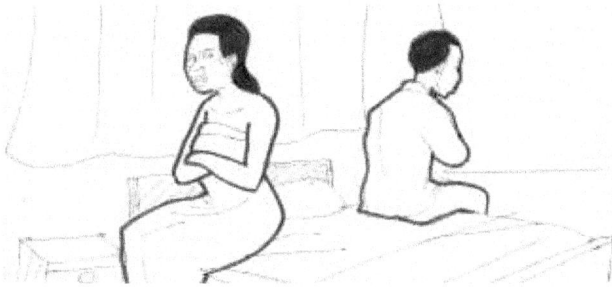

God cannot give His children anything but good things.

She later discovered that the pastor became impotent as an unbeliever while practicing homosexualism. It also became obvious that her husband could still be a practicing homosexual. That discovery made her lost hope in possible divine intervention for her husband's healing.

One thing led to another, and after three years of fruitless and painful marriage, she packed her things and left his house. The bad news is not that she left the husband, but that she left in bitterness against God for giving her that man and therefore finds it difficult to go to church again.

I explained to her that every good and perfect gift comes from God and that God cannot give His children anything but good things. We are still praying and believing God that she will be delivered from hatred induced by demons of homosexualism. It is only Satan and his fallen angels (demons) that thrive in hatred. My desire is that it will not become too late for the sister to repent.

CHAPTER SEVEN

IT IS DIFFICULT
TO RESIST!

"The eye of the adulterer waited for the twilight saying, no eye shall see me: and disguiseth his face" Job 24:15

The Longman family dictionary defines adultery as, "an act of voluntary sexual intercourse between a married person and somebody other than his/her spouse." Sexual relationship is sacred and is only right between married couples. Some people, especially men, believe that marriage is a license for them to sleep with whosoever they desire. This perverted understanding is the bedrock of rampant adulterous activities of married men with other married women or single ladies. This has contributed to a rise in cases of broken and polygamous marriages in our society today.

———∞———

Some people, especially men, believe that marriage is a
license for them to sleep with whosoever they desire.

———∞———

Our Lord Jesus while on earth had to resolve a case of adultery with wisdom. A woman was caught in an adulterous relationship, the man was let go and the woman was brought forward to be stoned to

104

death. Could a woman commit adultery without a man? Why did they not bring the man forward? Could it be that like in our days, people believe that men have the right after marriage to sleep with anybody they desire? The truth is, a married man has the right to sleep with only his wife.

> *"They say unto Him, master, this woman was taken in adultery, in the very act. ...when Jesus had lifted up Himself, and saw none but the woman, He said unto her, woman, where are those thine accusers? Hath no man condemned thee?" Jn.8:3-11.*

One of the reasons God instituted marriage was to prevent the sinful life of adultery or fornication. It was not God's intention to prevent fornication and with marriage promote the wicked act of adultery.

> *"Nevertheless, to avoid fornication, let every*

> *man have his own wife, and let every woman*
> *have her own husband" 1 Cor.7:2*

The prevalence of HIV/AIDS has brought to the fore the wicked and murderous nature of adultery and fornication. In Nigerian culture, women are at the receiving end. Consider the story of a married man who for the only reason that his wife was just then delivered of a baby and could not resume sexual intercourse immediately, took a willing woman other than his wife for sexual intercourse in

a hotel. Unknown to him, the woman in question was HIV positive. The married man contracted the HIV virus and was living with it unknowingly.

The truth is, a married man has the right to sleep with only his wife.

When their baby was weaned and he resumed sexual intercourse with the wife, the innocent woman contracted HIV virus too unknowingly.

The man eventually fell ill and was diagnosed HIV positive. His mind went to the only possible incident; his "one night stand" at the hotel. He was so ashamed and hid it from his wife until she was also diagnosed positive.

It was not God's intention to prevent fornication and with marriage promote the wicked act of adultery.

While the wife was crying in confusion on how she

could have contracted the disease, the husband broke down into tears and confessed his ordeal which he called "one night stand". He begged the wife to forgive him. He died some months later of complications from AIDS disease.

The wife had to bear the burden of raising their children alone and the challenges of the HIV/AIDS disease. She died some years later for what she knew nothing about; for the consequence of an adulterous "one night stand" of her late husband.

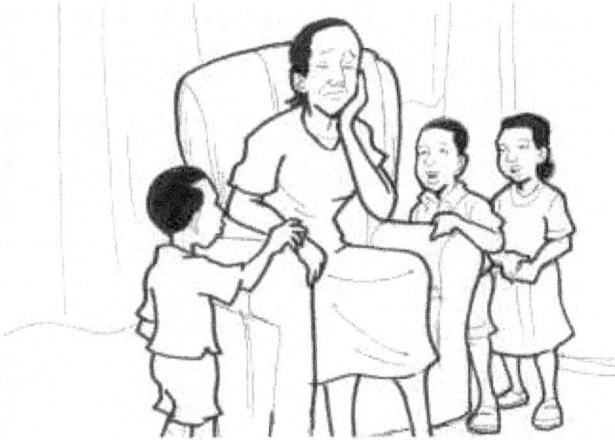

Some men are bold to give reasons why a woman can remain faithful while a man cannot. Some of the reasons include the following:

There are no plausible reasons to justify wickedness.

• **A man will have to wait for 9 months period of the wife's pregnancy without sexual intercourse.** This is not true. It is sheer ignorance on the part of the couple. Sex during pregnancy is allowed; only that care must be taken not to physically harm the baby in the womb.

109

♦ **A man must stay without sex after the wife puts to bed.** This is also not completely true. Doctors will counsel on the safest time and means to resume sexual relationship with your wife after delivery.

♦ **Abstinence is a family control method.** Abstinence is recommended for the unmarried and not for the married as a family planning method. We could consult our Doctors for other methods that will not expose either of the couple to the temptation of adultery.

♦ **The wife is not sexually active and strong; she is lazy in bed.** There are better ways to handle the situation as we will be told by our marriage counselors or Doctors.

♦ **My wife is wickedly starving me of sex.** We do not repay wickedness with wickedness. We should commit time to settle every quarrel in our marriage rather than finding solace in another woman that is not our wife.

———&———

Marriage cannot solve a lifelong internal conflict of lusting after everything on skirt.

———&———

There are no plausible reasons to justify wickedness. Adultery is not caused by anything outside the man who is engaged in it. The cause of adultery is from within a man.

> "...for from within, out of the heart of men proceedevil thoughts, adulteries, fornication, murders, ..." Mk.7:20-23.

Men, it is not caused by beautiful maids or sister-in-laws. You sneaked out of your matrimonial bedroom, away from your wife in the middle of the night and tried to rape that innocent girl. Even if the girl consents out of intimidation, it is still not her fault but the greedy spirit of lust inside of you.

111

> *"From whence come wars and fightings among you?*
> *Ye adulterers and adulteresses know ye not that the*
> *friendship of the world is enmity with God? ... "But*
> *every man is tempted, when he is drawn away of his*
> *own lust, and enticed. Then when lust hath*
> *conceived, it bringeth forth sin: and sin, when it is*
> *finished, bringeth forth death" Jam.4:1-4, 1:14-15.*

The spirit of lust is in the flesh. A carnal man will not be able to live above lust even after marriage. Men who believe that marriage will solve the lust problem are always surprised after marriage to discover that they are not satisfied with their beautiful wives. Marriage cannot solve a lifelong internal conflict of lusting after everything on skirt.

> *"But I say unto you, that whosoever looketh on a*
> *woman to lust after her hath committed adultery*
> *with her already in his heart" Matt.5:28.*

Flesh is humanity's fallen, corrupt or sinful nature

as distinguished from human nature, originally created by God. Flesh is man as he has allowed himself to become in contrast with man as God meant him to be. The solution to lust which is resident in the flesh cannot be found in the same flesh. The solution to the lust problem is found in the spirit.

> *"This I say then, walk in the spirit, and ye shall not fulfil the lust of the flesh" Gal. 5:16.*

I am not ashamed to confess that as a pastor, the extent to which I am victorious over lust is only to the extent that I submit my desires and internal conflicts to the control of the Holy Spirit. Without Jesus and by extension the enablement of the Holy Spirit, a pastor like me is as weak and gullible, wayward and useless, profane and perverse as every other man out there who has lost control of their senses because of anything in skirt.

—— ❧ ——

The solution to the lust problem is found in the spirit.

—— ❧ ——

It is not surprising then that some great men of God fell because of lust, fornication or adultery. The first amongst these men of God is Samson (Judg.16:4-21), second is David (2Sam. 11-12), and thirdly, is King Solomon1Ki.11, Neh.13:26). King Solomon in Prov.7:24-27, warns against the prostitute and the end of those who sin with her. He stressed that adultery is a destroyer of soul. It sounds like adultery is one of the weapons of Satan perfected for the destroying of the souls of men engaged in it. The adulterer in our story died of AIDS disease and so did his wife.

> *"But whosoever committeth adultery with a w o m a n*
> *lacketh understanding: he that doeth it destroyeth his*
> *own soul" Prov.6:32.*

114

The good news is that the Lord Jesus hates adultery but loves the adulterer. The truth is that the adulterer is one of those He died for on the cross. Jesus is waiting for the repentance of that adulterous prodigal son. He will, like the story of the prodigal son, restore all you may have lost including making you joint-heir with Him to enjoy His Father's great inheritance in heaven for eternity.

It is not surprising then that some great men of God fell because of lust, fornication or adultery.

Are you ready now to make that change happen by accepting Jesus as your Lord and Saviour? Then pray as follows:

God Almighty Father, I accept that I am a sinner and Jesus came and died for me. I accept Jesus into my life today. Cleanse me with the blood of Christ and write my name in your book of life. I refuse every covenant I have with the devil, directly or indirectly, in Jesus' name.

115

You are now a born again Christian. What you need now is a Bible, the great book that God will use to lead you on.

Part Three

DEFINING
HIV/AIDS

CHAPTER EIGHT

THE HIV/AIDS EPIDEMIC

In the worst AIDS-affected villages around Lake Victoria, numerous households include orphaned children. Some are cared for by relatives. Some find places in special programmes for orphans. And some fend for themselves, turning their hands to a variety of small enterprises sewing, cooking, goat-tending - to support themselves, and perhaps younger brothers and sisters.

The first case of AIDS in Nigeria was reported in 1986. Since then, HIV prevalence has steadily increased from 1.8% (1991) to 5.8% (2001) and a slight decline to 4.4% (2005). Selected Impacts as at 2005 is as follows:

♦ About 3.86 million people living with

HIV(PLWHIV)

♦ About 221,000 AIDS deaths

♦ About 1.3 million orphans

♦ About 370,000 new infections and

♦ About 540,000 in need of Anti - Retroviral (ARV) treatment

Although the prevalence rates appear low, Nigeria ranks third in terms of the actual number of people infected with HIV after India and South Africa. HIV infection began to spread in the 1970's. By early 1990, an estimated 6 million people throughout the world had been infected with HIV.

Cases of the AIDS disease and other clinical manifestations of HIV infection were reported in the United States of America in 1981. However, AIDS is known to have occurred in several other areas of the world before that by September 10, 1990, a total of 288,337 AIDS cases had been reported officially from Africa, the Americans, Asia, Europe and Oceania. AIDS develops only some years after a person acquires HIV infection, today's AIDS cases reflects the level of HIV infection 3 to 5 or even 10 years ago.

In contrast to most health problems, which affect either the very young or the elderly, AIDS affects mainly those in the active age group 20-49 years, by depriving the community of people in their most productive years. AIDS poses a serious threat to social and economic development and even to political stability.

Global HIV infections in 1993	
Mode of transmission	**Rate**
Sexual intercourse	70 - 80%
Mother to child	5 - 10%
Needle-sharing by drug users	5 - 10%
Blood transfusion	3 - 5%
Accidental needle-sticks to health care workers	less than 0.01%

122

CLINICAL MANIFESTATIONS

Pathogenesis:

HIV, the causative agent of AIDS, selectively infects specific white blood cells (CD4 cells) that are essential for the immune defense system. When the CD4 cells are destroyed, the infected person becomes susceptible to a range of opportunistic infectious diseases and cancer. AIDS is the term applied to a group of such conditions, the presence of which indicates severe damage to the immune system.

Rate of Progress to AIDS:

Initially it was thought that only a small proportion (5-10%) of HIV- infected persons would develop AIDS. Today, there is evidence that about 20% or more of those infected will develop AIDS within 5 years of becoming infected and about 50% within 10years. An increasing proportion will go on to develop AIDs after 10years, as people with HIV infection show progressive damage to their immune system over time. The case could be different with the use of currently available Anti-Retroviral drugs.

Manifestations:

The clinical signs and symptoms of HIV infection are many and varied. They include opportunistic infections and cancer as well as symptoms caused directly by HIV itself. The natural trend of HIV infection preceding the acute stage can be divided into 4 different stages, although all four do not necessarily occur in all infected individuals.

Acute Prodromal Manifestation

Acute HIV disease can occur as early as few weeks after the infection is acquired. It generally precedes the development of an anti-body response (seroconversion), which usually occurs in the first 6-12 weeks after infection. The period before development of anti-body response is often referred to as the window period; when the person is infectious but test for anti-body does not show it. Typical clinical manifestations in the acute phase are fever, lymphadenopathy, night sweats, skin rash, headache and cough.

STAGE 1

In this stage, the patient is either asymptomatic (not showing any symptoms) or with persistent lymphadenopathy. PGL is characterized by lymph node involving two or more sites, in the absence of any other current illness known to cause lymphadenopathy. It lasts for at least 3 months and slowly regresses during the course of the disease.

STAGE 2 (Early Disease):

This stage is characterized by the occurrence of typical mucocutaneous lesions like oral hairy Leukoplakia, Zoster and "constitutional" manifestations, such as moderate weight loss, fatigue, anorexia and night sweats are also common in this stage.

The types of opportunistic infections depend largely on the past and current exposure of the individual to microbial agents. This is the reason for the differences in the frequency of certain opportunistic infections between African and American or European HIV infected patients.

STAGE 3 (Intermediate disease):

The manifestations in this stage may occur more frequently sometime after the early symptoms but before the full development of Late-stage indicator disease. Stage 3 manifestations includes oral candidiasis, oral hairy leukoplakia, pulmonary tuberculosis, labial or genital herpes viral vesicular dermatitics, and some bacterial infections such as alveolar pneumonia, a fumour (Kaposi's sarcoma) and constitutional symptoms such as persistent fever, diarrhea, and weight loss exceeding 10% of body weight.

STAGE 4 (Late Disease):

In this stage the most commonly occurring opportunistic infections have a particular

severe course because of the profound immune suppression of the host. Commonly occurring infections may be protozoa (pneumonia, toxoplasmosis), fungal (visceral and oesophageal candidiasis), bacteria (salmonella septicaemia) or viral (cytomegalovirus, progressive multifocal leukoencephalitis).

Manifestations in Infants and Children:

A substantial proportion of infants who contact HIV infection from their mothers (before, during, or after birth) or possibly through breast feeding or from blood transfusion generally show symptoms by about 6-12 months of age

PHOTO: LOUISE GUBB

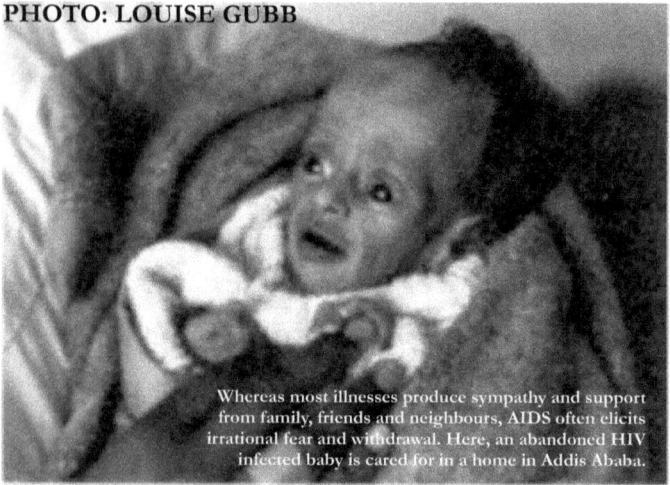

Whereas most illnesses produce sympathy and support from family, friends and neighbours, AIDS often elicits irrational fear and withdrawal. Here, an abandoned HIV infected baby is cared for in a home in Addis Ababa.

TRANSMISSION

HIV has been isolated from body fluids of infected persons, including saliva and tears. Only blood, semen, virginal secretions, and breast milk has been implicated in transmission. Epidemiological studies throughout the world have shown only three modes of HIV transmission, described below:

♦ Through sexual intercourse (from an infected person to his or her sexual partner or donated

128

semen). Sexual intercourse includes penetrative penis-vaginal, penis-anus, or oral-genital contact. (Sexual transmission)

♦ From exposure to blood, blood products or transplanted organs or tissues. Exposure to HIV infected blood may occur as a result of the transfusion of unscreened blood, the reuse of contaminated syringes and needles, e.g., by intravenous drug users.

(Parenteral transmission)

♦ From an infected mother to her fetus or infant, before, during, or shortly after birth.

(perinatal transmission)

HIV is not transmitted by the respiratory or enteric routes or by casual person-person contact in any setting, whether household, social, work, school, or prison. Nor is HIV transmitted by insects, food, water, toilets, swimming pools, shared eating and drinking utensils, or other objects such as second-hand clothing or telephones.

CHAPTER NINE

―――⟋⟍―――

FINALLY,
THE WAY OUT!

I almost left out the most important part of the book – the way out. For me, it was deliberate to focus only on how engaging in risky behaviours (sexual perversions) could heighten our exposure to HIV/AIDS disease. I did not set out to provide readers with an "almighty solution" to the different types of sexual perversion discussed in this book for that will be promising too much.

However, I reckon that, to show the people currently caught in the web of sexual perversions the way out, I must also show those not yet entangled the subtle ways many may have gotten themselves entrapped by Satan.

How Did I Get In?

The normal way into a house is through a door and surprisingly, the way out is also through a door. However, the thief enters a house through a window, broken down wall or roof and could enter through the door if allowed.

Our body communicates with its surrounding through five sensory organs. These organs act as one form of door or the other to the body. These organs could be doors or windows depending on what they are used for and who is using them; God or Satan. They include eyes, ears, nose, mouth and hands. Literally, these organs are important to the extent that they do not in their interaction with people and the environment become a door of offense. Spiritually, we are commanded in Matt.18:8-9 to do away with any habit, relationship

133

or church member that could become a leaven or agent of Satan to lead many astray. All the sense organs are intricately linked to the brain and to every part of the human body.

"Many members but yet one body…" (1Cor.12:16-21)

What we see

—❧—

…how many of us can sincerely say we will be unmoved by what we see with our eyes?

—❧—

Earlier in this book, you saw how I almost got lured into pornography via the internet. It was easy to shut down the computer and unsubscribe the internet service, but it was a spiritual warfare to get the images off my head. Now, If a pastor being used by God to save souls and touch lives can be thus tempted by the pictures I saw, how many of us can sincerely say we will be unmoved by what we see with our eyes?

The only man that was tempted but never fell or gave in to temptation is our Lord Jesus Christ. We can therefore draw strength from him to overcome when tempted.

The Way Out

The solution to preserving the eye window should include permanent locking. This is the hardest, most painful and also the most effective way of staying out of trouble. It means, for instance, refraining from all unhealthy sites online, reading of pornographic materials, watching of sexually explicit movies and lustfully looking at the back side of your beautiful sister-in-law or maid; the list is endless.

The above solution is a direct application of
"And if thine eye offend thee, pluck it out, and cast it from thee: ...Matt.18:9.
Sadly, this may be wrongly applied to the extreme by

asking people to throw away their television sets because of offensive music videos without considering the fact that it can be put to positive use. We need to be better informed on how to use the internet and filter it to block those offensive popup sites.

We must guard what we watch as movies and television channels must be carefully selected and for our children, carefully monitored and code protected. Like Job, you need to prayerfully covenant with your eyes not to think about any offensive material you may have seen with your eyes (Job 31:1).

Gifts or Bribery

───❧───

In being thankful to those who shower you with gifts, do not let their good gesture becloud your sense of judgment.

───❧───

Gifts are positive reinforcement while bribes are given to pervert judgment or get a favour. We are commanded in Ex. 23:8, *"not to accept a bribe because it blinds the wise and perverts the words of the righteous"*

The young girl in our story who was at home preparing for her examinations was blinded to the true intention of the businessman by gifts (bribes) he showered on her.

Another young man in one popular church was deceived into homosexualism by the special attention and gifts showered on him by a more matured man in the same church. One thing led to another and before he knew it, he was already having an affair with the more matured man. Like he said "it got to a point, I was the one looking for the man." He got so hooked that even when the matured man wanted the relationship to end, the young man refused.

137

The Way Out

The solution to the use of gifts as a form of bribery is proper orientation about gifts or the givers of those gifts. In being thankful to those who shower you with gifts, do not let their good gesture becloud your sense of judgment. Do not become emotionally attached to the gift or the giver when relating with them. It is a gift and not a loan to be repaid in kind.

A common warning to children is "do not accept gift from strangers". It is advisable to know from whom you receive gifts. Common sense will teach us to stop receiving gift from a giver whose intention and character is unknown. There is always a trade-off at the end of the transaction and there is hardly free lunch anywhere. Learn to be contented with what you have or what your parents can afford and if you must accept that gift, make sure it is a gift and not a bribe.

The Company We Keep

The elders have a saying that, 'evil association corrupts good manners.' Indeed, the best of morals can be corrupted by regular association with evil company. It is my opinion that nobody was born a drunkard, a drug addict, a lesbian, a gay or a prostitute. Nobody is born a black sheep of a family. Some who were born and raised with strong family values end up on the wrong side of life probably because of the company they kept at school or in their neighbourhood.

I remember how peer pressure landed me in a company of smokers and after months of outing together, I was coerced and mocked into lighting a stick of cigarette. I almost choked to death and my company told me it was always the experience of first timers. I ignored their encouragement and common sense taught me that smoking could stop my heart on the long run.

The Way Out

———⟨⟩———

It is my opinion that nobody was born a drunkard, a drug addict, a lesbian, a gay or a prostitute.

———⟨⟩———

As a teenager, I had to quit the company of rascals I was moving around with to deliver myself from the inevitable plunge into chain smoking and a life of addiction. Disconnection from pals is a difficult task because God created us to have fellowship with Him and our fellow men. Instead of total disconnect, we could relate with friends of questionable character at an arm's length to avoid partaking in their deeds. We can also follow up with them to help them.

Environmental influences

We are all born into different families. Our habits, character and other personality traits are formed within the family. Our families have helped to mould us into what we are now or what we would eventually become. There are different expectations for male and female children. For instance a female child is taught to speak softly, sit and walk like a lady, cook all known family menu and how to dress.

On the other hand, due to family indulgence, some children might turn out differently e.g. the tomboys. They are girls who dress, walk, speak and play like boys; eventually some turn out lesbians. I do not believe that anybody is born a tom boy and also do not agree that every tom boy will end up a lesbian. However, parents in bringing up their children must pay particular attention to values they bequeath to them.

The Way Out

...parents in bringing up their children must pay particular attention to values they bequeath to them.

There is need to evaluate every action through God's leading values. Good family values help children in forming the right opinion about his or her environment.

The Spiritual Dimension

There is a spiritual dimension to every problem on earth even the issues discussed in this book. This spiritual angle makes it impossible for common sense to be a solution. We must therefore explore spiritual dimensions to the things we do. The level of involvement in all the discussed behaviours is determined by the level of demonic possession and control over such individuals. Some may hear voices in their heads urging them on, others feel helplessly pushed and a few others feel they are in control of their senses while indulging in some of these behaviours.

The Way Out

A visit to a man of God for counseling or deliverance may just be all that will save the day for those under demonic control. Nature does not allow a vacuum and if a man is delivered of evil spirits (demons) and does not make an effort to be filled with the good spirit (Holy Spirit), the latter state of the fellow will be worse than the former. This is one of the reasons why some people may not believe in deliverance.

Think about it, you have nothing to lose by submitting yourself to deliverance and counseling.

Some preachers have been known to teach that once you are born again, you do not need to go for deliverance or counseling. This is a wrong teaching because the Lord Jesus Christ delivered men who were possessed by demons. Even Apostle Peter was possessed by Satan to discourage Jesus from going to the cross.

143

If believers cannot be possessed then why do we have lesbians, homosexuals, adulterers, fornicators and the likes right in our church whether pulpit or pew? It takes the indwelling or demonization of a man for him to do things that His God detests. It also takes God and His indwelling Holy Spirit to do those things that are pleasing to God. Think about it, you have nothing to lose by submitting yourself to deliverance and counseling.

Finally, for the benefit of those who are in need of a way of escape and those who are denying the possibility of ever getting involved in the behaviours described herein or of ever getting infected with HIV, love covers a multitude of sins. We must allow the love of God to transcend our prejudices. In the story of the three lesbians earlier in this book, my friend reached out to them with love and salvation was the result.

Appendix One

*Scarleteen "what you need to know
to wise up about HIV & AIDS"
by Heather Corinna*

You can spread AIDS through-

You might as well stop right there as you cannot spread AIDS to someone else at all. You can only spread HIV person-to-person. So, what IS HIV? And what is AIDS? Both are acronyms: HIV stands for Human Immunodeficiency Virus; AIDS for Acquired Immune Deficiency Syndrome. HIV is a virus people can and do spread around, and AIDS is a syndrome which people with HIV often eventually develop: HIV often progresses to AIDS and you cannot wind up with AIDS without having contracted HIV first. AIDS is not contagious, HIV is. Neither is currently curable. Once you have got HIV or AIDS, it is for life.

You have to have anal sex or do drugs to get HIV!

Unprotected anal intercourse (particularly for the receptive partner) and needle-sharing drug use are absolutely the two most prevalent risks of HIV for young people. But not only do those risks exist for people of all sexes and gender equally, especially as anal sex becomes more common among heterosexual teens, heterosexual vaginal intercourse is a very close second when it comes to HIV risks.

Understand that anal sex present an increased risk because anal and rectal tissue is more delicate than vaginal tissue, and more likely to have micro tears (incredibly small tears) or abrasions from sex, which present sites for infection. But the same can often be true with vaginal tissue, especially when we consider how many young people are having sex without lubricant, without responsive and gentle partners, and how common date and stranger rapes are for young women (forced or even consensual "rough" sex) increases risks of HIV and other STI transmission. Sexual violence plays a very big part in the HIV/AIDS pandemic.

HIV is spread through four routes, and most prevalently in this order: male sexual fluids, blood, female vaginal fluids or breast milk. If you are directly exposed to any of those things or expose others to them genitally, orally, or intravenously (in your veins) then you could get or spread HIV.

147

You'd have to have sex with a lot of people to get HIV.

Not at all! All you have to do is have unprotected sex with one person who has HIV. By all means, the greater number of sexual partners you have, the greater chance you've got of winding up with a partner with HIV, so limiting partners is a big help in reducing the risk of HIV. But if you're having unsafe sex with even one partner, you're at risk, so it's a very big deal to never make exceptions when it comes to safe sex, not even just "that once."

What is PEP?

You may not know about it, but much like we have the morning-after pill to help prevent pregnancy once we've already had a risk, there is also similar "morning-after" treatment for those who have been exposed to the HIV virus, called Post-Exposure Prophylaxis (PEP). Studies show PEP has reduced the risk of HIV infection by 81 percent in health-care workers involved in needle-stick accidents. PEP is not available everywhere or to just everyone. It is primarily used for health-care workers, but is also sometimes now used for pregnant women or rape victims known or strongly suspected to have been exposed to the virus. Ideally, it should be used within just a couple of hours after exposure, and is no longer suggested once 72 hours have passed.

You can tell who has HIV and AIDS: it makes you look really scary, right?

Most people with HIV look just like most people without HIV. HIV positive people usually look no different than anyone else; not facially, not genitally. A whole lot of people with HIV, including people who don't know they have it and aren't being treated for it feel and look just fine most of the time. HIV is often asymptomatic (it shows no symptoms) and when symptoms are present, they're a whole lot like just having the flu. Those who have symptoms from HIV experience things like fevers, chronic yeast infections, easy bruising, body rashes, chronic fatigue, diarrhea or weight loss. It is really easy to think you've got something else or nothing at all when you acquire HIV, especially at first.

149

When HIV progresses to AIDS, we would be lying if we said that AIDS patients looked picture perfect. People with AIDS are very seriously ill and often look just as seriously ill as they are. Regardless, just like with any other STI, thinking you can know if and when someone has an STI just by looking is a really stupid thing to think. You can't know a person's STI status based on how they look.

But you don't even have to ask for HIV tests anymore; your doctor usually does them at regular checkups.

While many general practitioners and clinics have upped their efforts to make HIV screenings more routine, it's never smart to assume you've been tested without finding out for sure. Too, a lot of doctors report that because of the cultural climate in terms of teens and sex, they are nervous to ask teens about their sexual activity and STI testing. It's often estimated that less than 20% of teens and young adults in the U.S. with HIV have been tested and are aware that they have it.

There's no reason not to be proactive and double check with your healthcare provider that you have been tested for HIV. If you have been sexually active and don't want to tell your doctor (something we wouldn't advise keeping to yourself from healthcare pros, but still), you don't have to disclose that: you can ask for a test without discussing your sexual history at all. If your doctor asks why you're asking for testing, all you need to say is because you want to be sure you don't have HIV.

I can't get tested, because when you do, the doctor or clinic has to notify everyone you know.

That's a reasonable fear, as there's so much stigma around HIV, and with young people who usually acquire HIV through drug use or sex, people knowing you've got HIV often also means people knowing (or guessing about) what you did whatever it was to wind up with HIV. But that's a fear which isn't grounded in the reality of HIV testing right now.

You can get a test for HIV, an oral swab and/or a blood test at your regular general doctor's office or general health clinic, at a hospital, via student health services or through your gynecologist, urologist or sexual health/family planning clinic. There are also clinics which specifically deal with HIV testing and treatment, too. But ALL of those places are legally obligated to protect your privacy.

I don't want to even go INTO an HIV or AIDS clinic to get tested, because if I don't have it already, I might get it there.

Not anything close to likely. Again, there are four major routes of HIV transmission, and if you're not having unprotected sex with anyone in the clinic, sharing needles with anyone in the clinic (and clinicians are beyond impeccable about using clean needles for testing), or breastfeeding from someone in the clinic, you're not going to wind up with HIV. You can't get HIV through casual contact -- like sitting on the same chair or sharing a toilet and you also can't get it from even pretty close contact with someone who is HIV positive. Close contact like closed-mouth kissing, hugging, handshaking and even sharing glasses or cups, don't present HIV risks.

So, how can you protect yourself?

The most effective way to avoid acquiring HIV is to abstain from vaginal and anal sex with partners (oral sex may present risks, especially if and when blood is involved, but oral sex presents greater STI risks with other STIs than it does with HIV), injection drug use and any exposure to other people's blood in other contexts (such as in unclean tattoo parlors or via self-done tats, by sharing razors or toothbrushes, or via scenarios like biting or being bitten).

What if I get a test and find out I'm positive?

No one is going to play Pollyanna and say that getting a positive result is going to be your best day ever. That's tremendously tough news for anyone and there's little to soften that blow. But the sooner you find out, the better off you are, and the sooner you can get started on taking care of yourself as best you can. Again, being positive really, truly, is not a death sentence anymore, nor does it mean your whole life is over. People who are HIV-positive now and who get good treatment and take good care of themselves and those around them can have

153

excellent relationships including sexual relationships, get pregnant and have kids, keep their jobs, and achieve the goals they aspire to. That's not to say all of that is always easy as pie, it's often not, but it is doable, and all the more so when you face things head-on, and don't delay in getting diagnosed and treated.

There's just no good reason to avoid getting tested regularly. If you find out you don't have HIV, that's one less thing for you to have to worry about. If you find out you do, the sooner you know, the better off you and everyone around you will be, and the better your chances for getting through it and being able to continue the life you're just starting in the healthiest way possible.

Appendix Two

HIV & AIDS Voluntary Counseling
& Testing Services Centres

There are several testing centres in strategic places across the nation. Some of these centres are:

1. Salvation Army Headquarters ANNEX,
    Voluntary Counseling &Testing Centre
    11, Odunlami Street, by CMS bookshop, Broad street,
    Lagos Tel: +234 803 300 9098, +234 802 360 9707,
    +234 1-2633556.
2. Society for women and AIDS in Africa/Nigeria (SWAAN)
    Voluntary Counseling and Testing Centre,
    No 4 Barde road, by Polo Ground,
    Independence Road, Kano, Kano State.
    Tel: +234 64-663428, +234 803-3279027.
3. Prevention of Mother-to-child-transmission (PMTCT) Edo State,
4. University of Benin Teaching Hospital (UBTH)
5. Irrua Specialist teaching hospital, Irrua
6. St. Philomena hospital, Benin city

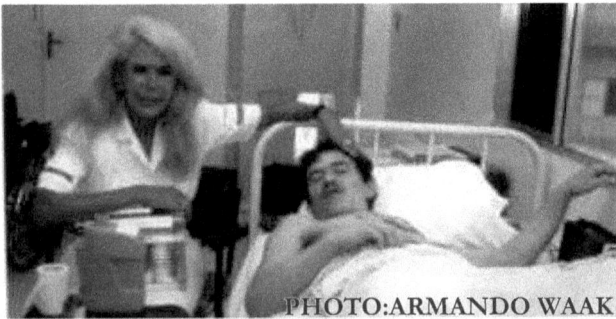

PHOTO:ARMANDO WAAK

CARE & SUPPORT SERVICES

Below are societies that offer care and support services:

a) Society for women and aids in Africa (Nigeria) Home based care and support services Voluntary counseling and testing centre, 12, Apena street , off Cole street, Ojuelegba, Surulere, Lagos. Tel: +234 1-5837618

b) Society for women and aids in Africa (Nigeria)
Home based care and support services
Voluntary counseling and testing ctr. centre,
4, Barde road, by polo ground Independent Rd;
Kano State. Tel: +234 64-663428, +234 803-3279027.

c) AIDS Alliance in Nigeria
Psychosocial Support/ Media Advocacy
26, Igbosere Rd, Lagos Island
Help lines: +234 1-4861715, +234 1 4727902,
+234 803327449, +234 8023331032.

d) Living hope care, Danaija Ajanaku House,
Isokun, Ilesa, Osun State +234 36-46099, +234 36-461015

VOLUNTARY COUNSELLING & TESTING CENTRE (VCT)
Lagos State (VCT Centers)
Ajeromi General Hospital
Apapa General Hospital
Badagry General Hospital
Epe General Hospital
Gbagada General Hospital
Ikeja General Hospital
Ikorodu General Hospital
Island General Hospital
Isolo General Hospital
Massey Children's Hospital
Alimosho primary health care
Ebutte metta primary health care
Mushin primary health care

KANO State (VCT Centers)
Danbaba General Hospital
Gwarzo General Hospital
Infectious disease hospital
Kura General Hospital

157

Aminu kano Teaching Hospital
Murtala Muhammed Hospital
Wudil general Hospital

ANAMBRA STATE (VCT Centers)

Akwa General Hospital
Nnamdi Azikwe teaching hospital
Our ladies of Lourdes, Ihiala
St. charles Borromeo, onitsha
Ekulobia General Hospital

TARABA State (VCT Centers)

Jalingo speciallist Hospital
Federal Capital Territory   (VCT Centers)
National Hopsital Abuja
Gwagwalada specialist hospital
St. mary's catholic Hospital gwagwalada
Wuse general hospital

FOR SPIRITUAL COUNSELLING

E-mail: Gloriousbirth_2004@yahoo.co.uk
Or call +234 8023220158 for an appointment.

BIBLIOGRAPHY

a) National Agency for the Control of AIDS,
    "Nigeria UNGASS Report, 2007"

b) World Health Organization, Geneva, "Guidelines for
    Counseling about HIV infections and Disease"

c) World Health Organization, Geneva , "AIDS images of the
    epidemic"

d) Heather Corinna, "what you need to know to wise up about
    HIV & AIDS" Scarleteen

e) Dr. ED Murphy " The Hand Book for Spiritual Warfare"

To contact Pastor Anthony Amalokwu, write:

Anthony Amalokwu

R.C.C.G. – Glorious Liberty Assembly

192, Kirikiri Road (near Oceanic Bank), Olodi-Apapa, Lagos.

E-Mail: anthonyamalokwu@yahoo.com, Website: http://pastorthony.blogspot.Com

Please include your prayer requests and comments when you write.

To book Pastor Tony for speaking engagements, please call: 08023220158, 07092293865.

www.ingramcontent.com/pod-product-compliance
Lightning Source LLC
Chambersburg PA
CBHW060755050426
42449CB00008B/1421